W9-BRV-586

WITHDRAWN

Archie, Peyton, and Eli Manning

Football's Royal Family

Jeanne Nagle

New York

WEST PALM BEACH PUBLIC LIBRARY
411 CLEMATIS STREET
WEST PALM BEACH , FL. 33401
(561) 868-7700

For football, and Manning, fans everywhere

Published in 2010 by The Rosen Publishing Group, Inc.
29 East 21st Street, New York, NY 10010

Copyright © 2010 by The Rosen Publishing Group, Inc.

First Edition

All rights reserved. No part of this book may be reproduced in any form without permission in writing from the publisher, except by a reviewer.

Library of Congress Cataloging-in-Publication Data

Nagle, Jeanne.
Archie, Peyton, and Eli Manning: football's royal family / Jeanne Nagle.
   p. cm. (Sports families)
Includes bibliographical references and index.
ISBN 978-1-4358-3550-4 (library binding)
ISBN 978-1-4358-8518-9 (pbk)
ISBN 978-1-4358-8519-6 (6 pack)
1. Manning, Archie, 1949– 2. Manning, Peyton. 3. Manning, Eli, 1981– 4. Manning family. 5. Football players—Biography. I. Title.
GV939.A1N34 2010
796.33092—dc22
[B]

2009024833

Manufactured in the United States of America

CPSIA Compliance Information: Batch #LW10YA: For Further Information contact Rosen Publishing, New York, New York at 1-800-237-9932

On the cover: Left: New York Giants quarterback Eli Manning (number 10) surveys the field during a game. Center: New Orleans Saints quarterback Archie Manning (number 8), the Manning family patriarch, rolls out to pass. Right: Indianapolis Colts quarterback Peyton Manning (number 18) sets up for a pass. The Mannings have become one of professional football's most respected families.

On the back cover: NASCAR is a registered trademark of the National Association for Stock Car Auto Racing, Inc.

Contents

A jubilant Eli Manning, quarterback of the New York Giants, holds up the Vince Lombardi Trophy after the Giants defeated the New England Patriots in the Super Bowl in 2008. With this win, Eli cemented his reputation in the NFL and his place in the Manning family football dynasty.

To Archie Manning, the moment must have been like a joyful case of déjà vu, which is when present events seem as if they've happened before. Standing in a crowded football stadium, with confetti raining down and cheering fans everywhere, Manning watched as his quarterback son received the 2008 Most Valuable Player (MVP) award for leading his team to a Super Bowl victory.

The truth is, there was no déjà vu involved. Manning actually had lived through this moment just the year before. The only difference was that there had been another first name engraved on the game's MVP trophy. In 2007, his middle son, Peyton, had won the award after leading the Indianapolis Colts to the National Football League (NFL) championship. Now he had the privilege of celebrating as his youngest son and Peyton's little brother, Eli, took home a Super Bowl ring and MVP honors.

Seeing your sons reach such heights in their chosen careers would be a proud moment for any father. Watching Peyton and then Eli succeed at the sport of professional football was especially touching for Archie, though. That's because football is the family business. The Manning boys had followed in their father's footsteps when they entered the NFL. After four years as a college football star, Archie had spent 15 years as a quarterback in the pros. Despite lots of personal talent, he had never played for a team that made it to the Super Bowl. For Archie, seeing his sons being crowned champions was the next best thing to actually winning the big game himself.

Because their dad had been a talented and well-respected professional football player, it might seem as if Peyton and Eli were expected to become football superstars. Archie claims otherwise. "I never thought about them even playing college ball, much less pro football, much less winning Super Bowls or MVPs," he told reporters after the New York Giants' win in 2008. "It wasn't in the plan. We tried to raise kids just like other parents raised their kids. I can't explain it."

Fate, obviously, had other plans. Raw talent for throwing the ball, as well as the ability to see the entire field and make plays, seem to run in the family. Combine that with a strong work ethic and a love of the game that Archie had instilled in his boys and it's no wonder that Peyton and Eli have been so successful. The result is a legacy that's rarely matched in professional sports. Today, the Mannings have become the country's royal family of football.

Chapter One

STARTING OUT

The story of the Manning family football dynasty began in a small southern town. Born in 1949, Elisha Archie Manning III grew up in Drew, Mississippi. His father, who was called Buddy, ran a machinery shop in the farming community. His mother, Jane, worked as a legal secretary. Young Archie was something of a sports fanatic. He participated in every organized sport that Drew had to offer. Baseball was his favorite, but he also ran track and played basketball and, of course, football.

Archie's first real experience on the football field came when he tried out for the town's peewee league as a fifth grader. He played running back that year but was also interested in being the team's quarterback. In sixth grade, he became a peewee quarterback. From then on, it was the only position he ever played in the sport.

Being a quarterback was so much fun for Archie that he wanted to play football all the time. In fact, in the eighth grade, he was the quarterback on two separate teams. He played as a starter on his junior high school team and kept on leading the peewee squad as well. That arrangement didn't last long, though. Peewee football is generally for children who do not play for a school team. It's like the difference between amateur and professional players. The parents of children on opposing teams complained, and Archie was taken off the peewee roster. He was disappointed but could then concentrate on the junior high team.

HIGH SCHOOL STANDOUT

Injuries sidelined Archie for large portions of his college career, but they did not dim the promise he showed while on the field.

Archie continued as a multisport athlete as he entered high school. He represented his school on the basketball, baseball, track, and football teams. In the ninth grade, he was named backup quarterback on the varsity squad. He was thrilled to be second-string to his hometown sports hero, James Hobson. Partway into the season, the coach told Archie he was going to let him run a play during the next game. Right before his big break on the field, however, he suffered a break of another kind. A broken right arm dashed Archie's hopes of playing in the game and also ended his season early that year.

When he became a sophomore, Archie thought about quitting football. The aches and pains of playing were beginning to take their toll on him. It wasn't until the team's new head coach told him he was Drew High School's "quarterback of the future" that Archie decided to stick with the sport. After Hobson had graduated, Archie became the starting quarterback of the school's varsity team in his junior year. During the third game of the season, he broke his left arm and was out for the rest of the year.

Archie didn't let his injuries discourage him, however. He came back the next season and played even stronger. Archie's senior year was noteworthy for two reasons. First, he managed to play his entire senior year

Peyton was a standout quarterback at Isidore Newman High School in New Orleans, Louisiana, where he led the team to three consecutive winning seasons.

without getting injured. Second, he caught the attention of college scouts, earning a full scholarship to the University of Mississippi. Also called Ole Miss, the university is located in Oxford, Mississippi.

THE NEXT GENERATION

Peyton Williams Manning grew up playing football. Born in 1976 in New Orleans, Louisiana, he began tossing the football around as a toddler, playing catch with his older brother, Cooper. When the boys were in the locker room of the New Orleans Saints, which was the team that Archie played

ONE MANNING MORE

Professional football fans may have had another Manning to admire if it hadn't been for a single medical diagnosis. Archie's oldest son, Cooper, was a fine athlete in his own right. He played wide receiver at Isidore Newman in New Orleans, catching passes thrown by Peyton during his last two years on the team. An All-State player in high school, Cooper was set to play ball at his father's alma mater, Ole Miss.

His fortunes changed, however, when he was diagnosed with spinal stenosis, a narrowing of the spine that causes numbness and pain. Cooper had surgery on his spine when he was 18 years old. Afterward, he had to learn to walk all over again. His football career was over.

Cooper has been realistic about his situation. "I really never had any bitterness," he told a reporter for *USA Today* in 2008. "I just said, this is the hand I'm dealt and I'm going to play it."

for, they would form balls out of wads of athletic wrapping tape. They would throw the tape to each other, pretending to make big plays.

Peyton had the advantage of learning football strategy from his father, which is something that Archie never got from Buddy. Archie let his sons watch Saints game films with him. The older man would point out not only what he did as a quarterback, but also how the defense of the other teams would react.

As interested as he was in his dad's professional career, Peyton was absolutely fascinated with college ball. He was a big fan of the Southeastern Conference (SEC), which included his dad's alma mater, Ole Miss. Peyton would repeatedly listen to audiotapes of his dad's college games. He memorized his father's plays, and on the family's front lawn, he would act out those moments, with himself as the quarterback in place of Archie. He even gave a commentator's play-by-play description of the action, out loud, as he went through his paces.

Peyton's first experience with organized football was with the Greenies of Isidore Newman, a private school in New Orleans. Students may attend Newman from kindergarten through high school. He started playing football in the seventh grade. His position, of course, was starting quarterback. Like his father, Peyton played other sports as well. He was on Newman's basketball and baseball teams, too. Even as busy as he was with sports, he still managed to pull good grades.

As the starter on Newman's varsity football team, beginning in the tenth grade, Peyton led his school to winning seasons each year. As a senior, he led Newman to the state semifinals in 1991. That same year, he was named the Gatorade Circle of Champions National Player of the Year. The exciting thing was that playing for Newman was just the beginning of an illustrious career in football for Peyton Manning.

ALONG COMES ELI

Five years after Peyton was born, Archie and his wife, Olivia, had another son, Elisha Nelson Manning. Like his brothers, Eli was born in New Orleans. While Peyton and Cooper were a lot like their dad, Eli took after his mother. He had her easygoing manner, which earned him the nickname "Easy."

The older boys were able to spend a lot of time with their father as kids because they lived in the same town in which Archie played ball. But when Eli was growing up, Archie was playing and living in other towns. Games of football on the front lawn with dad weren't as frequent in those days.

Consequently, Eli looked up to his big brothers. Cooper and Peyton let him join them during their family football games. Yet the youngest Manning very rarely got to play quarterback. The older boys took turns pretending to be their father, while Eli was stuck playing center or receiver. Because of

The Manning family is a very tight-knit group. Seated clockwise from back left in this 1996 photo are Cooper, Olivia, Archie, Eli, and Peyton.

his mellow nature, "Easy" Manning never put up a fuss about not being allowed to throw the ball.

Peyton had another way of teaching his little brother a thing or two about football. He used to pin Eli down and quiz him about SEC teams. Every time Eli got an answer wrong, Peyton would punch him. Needless to say, Eli soon learned to answer correctly.

Eli began his schooling at Isidore Newman, just like Cooper and Peyton before him. When it was discovered that he had difficulty reading, Eli was transferred to a smaller school for a few years so that he could get extra attention. He returned to Newman when he started eighth grade and quickly joined the junior varsity football team. Eli didn't start out playing quarterback, but his skills in that position quickly became apparent. Under Eli's leadership, the Newman Greenies went to the state quarterfinals two years in a row, in 1997 and 1998.

Chapter Two

ON THE RIGHT PATH

Going away to college is an exciting and important time in a young adult's life for a number of reasons. First, there is the opportunity to train and gain the skills necessary for a career. Meeting new people—those with similar interests, as well as those with different backgrounds and beliefs who offer new ways of looking at the world—is another advantage. Many folks also enjoy the sense of freedom and independence they feel while away at school.

For athletes, college is significant for another reason, too. Participating in college-level sports is the surest way to get the attention of professional sports teams and agents. There are a lucky few who become pro athletes right out of high school. But most players are recruited, or chosen to play pro sports, based on their performance in college.

Such was the case for Archie, Peyton, and Eli Manning. Adding to their excellent records while playing for junior high and high school teams, each man assured himself a spot in the NFL because of his play on the university football field.

A SOUTHERN LEGEND

Not only did Archie Manning enjoy playing the game, he also hoped that football would get him into college. An athletic scholarship was his best

An Ole Miss Rebel and star quarterback for three years, Archie is seen here passing in a 1969 game. He won many awards, including Mississippi Sportsman of the Year and the Nashville Banner Trophy as Most Valuable Player in the Southeastern Conference.

hope of being able to afford the tuition. Three colleges wound up recruiting him to play for their teams. Archie chose to attend Ole Miss.

As the starting quarterback for three years for the Ole Miss Rebels, Archie racked up many records and awards. Among his accomplishments is tying the SEC record for total yards in one game, against the University of Alabama. Making the victory even sweeter was the fact that the contest was the first televised college football game. As recalled in the autobiography *Manning*, Bear Bryant, Alabama's renowned head football coach, told the press that Archie was "the most athletic quarterback I've ever seen."

Archie was well-loved at Ole Miss. When he graduated, the school retired his number, which means that no one else will ever play for the university wearing that number again. Retiring a number is quite an honor. Archie's number is the only one ever retired by the school. The

FAMILY TRAGEDY

The Manning family football dynasty was almost over before it had even started. While Archie was playing for the University of Mississippi, his father committed suicide. Worried about who would take care of his mother and sister, Archie planned to quit school and get a job. Quitting school would also mean quitting football and any chance he had of being drafted by a professional team. Without their dad as a role model, Peyton and Eli might have pursued careers other than professional sports.

Fortunately, Archie's mom wouldn't hear of him quitting school. Jane Manning convinced her son that the family would be fine. She persuaded Archie to go back to school. His skills at Ole Miss caught the attention of professional scouts and got him drafted into the NFL.

admiration for Archie Manning and all he did for Ole Miss football continues. Mississippi native and best-selling author John Grisham has called Archie "a legend larger than life." A character in Grisham's novel *The Pelican Brief* is named after the Manning family patriarch. And to this day, the speed limit on the University of Mississippi campus is 18, in honor of his player number.

DIFFERENT SCHOOL, SAME GREAT RESULTS

Recruiters from many top teams enthusiastically pursued Peyton Manning. Most people figured he would accept the University of Mississippi's offer. If Cooper had been a wide receiver for the Rebels, as he had planned before his medical issues arose, Peyton would probably have gone to Ole Miss. The chance to play with his brother again, as they had at Newman, would have sealed the deal. But because Cooper was permanently sidelined and not playing football, Peyton decided instead to attend the University of Tennessee in Knoxville in 1994.

In his freshman year, Peyton became the starting quarterback for the Tennessee Volunteers after injuries had sidelined the team's original starter and that player's backup. After losing three of their first four games that season, the Vols turned things around and lost only one game under Peyton's leadership. His excellence on the field won him many honors, including one that must have been extra special to him. The coaches in his team's conference made him an All-SEC first-team pick and named him SEC Freshman of the Year. In only his first year, Peyton had been named one of the finest players in his beloved SEC.

Throughout his sophomore and junior years, Peyton became something of a hero on the Tennessee campus and within the city of Knoxville. Fellow students asked him for autographs, and they often cheered when he walked into a room. The Knoxville Zoo even named a baby giraffe after him. Like his father at Ole Miss, Peyton remains popular at Tennessee. The Vols

Peyton received a special honor commemorating his outstanding career as a University of Tennessee Volunteer. His college jersey number 16 was officially retired.

retired his number, 16, in 2005. And a street that leads to the campus football stadium has been named Peyton Manning Pass.

MAKING A BIG DECISION

After three seasons at Tennessee, Peyton had thrown for 53 touchdowns and more than 7,000 yards. The Volunteers had three winning seasons and two Citrus Bowl victories while Peyton was in charge of running their offense. Needless to say, those statistics made him a hot prospect in the eyes of the NFL. Many teams started making him offers to play for them right away, even before his senior year of college.

The chance to make millions of dollars and play professional football must have been very tempting. Yet in the end, Peyton decided to stay in school and play for the Vols one more year. He said he wanted to slow down and simply enjoy life as a college senior. "Money can't buy the memories, friendships, and tradition," he told a reporter from *Boy's Life* magazine about his decision to stick it out at Tennessee.

An interesting fact is that Peyton could have graduated at the end of his junior year. By taking extra courses, he had earned a degree in speech communication in just three years. His decision to stay for a fourth year was based on principle, rather than needing to earn class credits. He wound up taking graduate school courses during his fourth year at the university.

Eli extended his playing days at Ole Miss by a year, capping his college career with a phenomenal final season. Eli is seen here throwing a pass during the Rebels' defeat of the Oklahoma State Cowboys in the Cotton Bowl in 2004.

ANOTHER MANNING AT OLE MISS

Eli's strong performances week in and week out as Newman's starting quarterback resulted in a lot of attention from college scouts. Eli may have had a personality like his mother's, but when it came to football, he definitely took after his father. He decided to attend school and play ball at the University of Mississippi in 1999.

Unlike Peyton, Eli didn't become a starter his freshman year. In fact, he didn't see any playing time at all his first year at Ole Miss. The head coach decided to redshirt him for a season. This meant that Eli could practice with the team but could not play in any games. Redshirting is a way for coaches to bring players along slowly. Because college athletes are allowed to play varsity sports for four years, the move also meant that Eli could stay an extra year at the university and play ball, if he chose to do so.

He spent most of his sophomore year on the bench as well, as a backup quarterback. Made starter in his junior year, Eli led the Rebels to a 7–4 season, including a seven-overtime, two-point loss to Arkansas. The next season, the team broke even at 6–6, despite impressive numbers by Eli.

By this time, he had a decision to make. Because he had been redshirted his freshman year, Eli could stay and play during the 2003 season. The team's record the year before had been disappointing. Also, Eli had hoped to do something that even his Ole Miss legend of a father had not accomplished—win the SEC championship. He wound up staying at the university for a fifth year.

That turned out to be a smart move. Eli had a fantastic season, passing for 3,600 yards and 29 touchdowns. While the Rebels just missed going to the SEC championship game, they did finish the season with a 10–3 record and a Cotton Bowl win. That year's performance earned Eli plenty of awards and greatly increased his standing in the 2003 NFL Draft.

Chapter Three

GOING PRO AND CAREER HIGHLIGHTS

Each year, sports journalists present the Heisman Trophy, which is an award given to the most outstanding college football player. Oddly enough, none of the Mannings ever won the Heisman. In 1969, Archie received the fourth-highest number of votes. The following year, he had the third-most votes. Coming in fourth and third may not seem like a big deal. But keep in mind that Archie was up against thousands of college players, not just quarterbacks. And he was in the top five two years in a row.

Peyton came in sixth in Heisman voting after his first year of play. It seemed like a sure thing for him to win the award after his senior year in 1997. However, many in the sports world were shocked when University of Michigan cornerback Charles Woodson took home the trophy instead.

At Archie's request, Ole Miss did not push Eli as a Heisman candidate during his junior year. Archie knew how distracting the race for the award had been for Peyton in 1997, and he wanted Eli to concentrate on his schoolwork and football instead. All bets were off the next year, however. Eli was the second runner-up in 2003 Heisman voting.

As it turns out, the Heisman has been just about the only award the Mannings have not received during their careers. From Super Bowl rings to being named MVPs in the league, Archie, Peyton, and Eli have been honored in countless other ways.

Drafted out of college by the New Orleans Saints, Archie played hard but never quite made the type of impact in the NFL that his sons have. Archie is seen here scrambling upfield during a game against the Los Angeles Rams.

THE FIRST TO ENTER THE NFL

The very first achievement for each man was earning a spot on a professional football team. Each year, pro teams choose players during the NFL draft. Eligible college players—mostly seniors—are grouped together in a pool, and NFL franchises pick who they want to join their team. The team with the worst record during the previous season picks first. There are seven rounds in the draft, which means that each team gets to pick seven players. The best players get picked in the first two rounds.

Archie was the second player chosen in the first round in the 1971 draft, by the New Orleans Saints. The Saints were a struggling team in need of a strong leader. They picked Archie in the hopes that he would make everybody around him better. It didn't work out that way, unfortunately. Complicating matters was the fact that Archie was prone to injury in the pros, just as he had been in high school. In 1976, his passing arm was operated on twice for extreme tendonitis. Archie wound up sitting on the bench that entire season.

When he was healthy and on the field, Archie played well during his 11 years with the Saints. However, sports journalists and others who follow football believe that he never had a combination of quality players who could win games. Archie also played for the Houston Oilers and the Minnesota Vikings. Neither of those teams ever made it close to playing in the Super Bowl either.

TURNING THINGS AROUND

The Indianapolis Colts made Peyton the number one overall draft pick in 1998. That means that he was the first pick in the first round—the most desired player in the draft. In honor of his father, Peyton chose the same jersey number, 18, that Archie had at Ole Miss.

Peyton was put in charge of the Colts' offense right away. Still, the team struggled defensively and ended the season with a losing record of 3–13. The team's young quarterback seemed to take that poor showing as a challenge. Peyton worked extra hard on strategy and put in extra time practicing with his receivers. Between that and a beefed-up defense, the Colts managed to flip the numbers on the previous year's record, winning 13 games and losing only 3. This was the greatest turnaround in NFL history.

Since then, the Colts have had nothing but winning seasons. Peyton was able to accomplish what his father hadn't been able to with the Saints. He had taken a consistently losing team and made them winners. Although he

A losing season during his rookie year with the Indianapolis Colts only encouraged Peyton to sharpen his skills. The result was the greatest turnaround in NFL history.

didn't do it alone, Peyton was given most of the credit for the team's turn-around. People refer to him as a "franchise player." A franchise player is a person around whom an entire team is built. In other words, the entire Colts organization depends on Peyton to keep the team on track and winning.

A BUMPY START

Six years after Peyton went to the Colts, it was Eli's turn in the draft. The San Diego Chargers had the first pick in 2004, and they made Eli the number one pick overall. Apparently, Eli wasn't thrilled to be playing for the Chargers. Shortly after the pick was made, he called a press conference. He said that he was thinking about going to law school instead of playing for the Chargers.

What hardly anyone knew at the time was that the Chargers had made a deal with the New York Giants. The Giants traded their first-round draft pick, Phil Rivers, and a couple of other players to San Diego for Eli. Once the deal was announced, Eli put aside his plans for law school and became a backup quarterback to starter Kurt Warner for the Giants.

Eli became the Giants' starter in 2005. His first season in charge was rocky. He threw for 24 touchdowns but nearly as many interceptions.

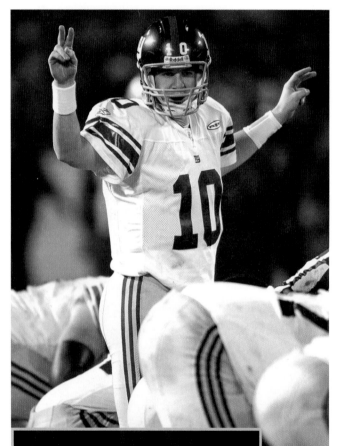

Thanks to a draft trade, Eli wound up in a New York Giants uniform in 2004. His first pro start was the following year.

A FAMILY AFFAIR

The Mannings have also been honored as a family. The Mississippi State Legislature proclaimed that March 10, 2009, was Manning Day. Each member of the family, including Cooper and Olivia, was honored for his or her service to the state, both on and off the football field. The family has made an impact on the state and throughout the South through community service work.

When the Giants were defeated by the Carolina Panthers in the first round of the playoffs that year, fans and the media began to question Eli's ability to lead the team. Going into the 2007 season, the doubts continued. Then Eli and the Giants took their play up a notch and won enough games to get them into the playoffs. His performance in the playoffs, all the way through to winning the conference, silenced his critics. Eli had proven himself a talented, capable, and winning NFL quarterback.

CHAMPIONSHIP SEASONS

As a player, Archie Manning never made it to the NFL playoffs, let alone the Super Bowl. His sons, however, didn't have that problem. Peyton was the first to break through into the playoffs. In Peyton's 11 seasons, the Colts have made it to the playoffs 9 times. For the most part, the team never made it past the first round in the early days, with the exception of the 2003 season. That year, the Colts made it to the conference title game. Teams need to win their conference title before they can go on to the Super Bowl.

The Colts' poor playoff record was forgotten three years later, when the team finally made it to the Super Bowl. In the title game win against the Chicago Bears, Peyton completed 25 of 38 passes, gained 247 passing yards, and threw for a touchdown. He later told reporters that the victory was a team effort. Yet his contributions to the win were rewarded with the game's MVP award.

Eli's Super Bowl experience was perhaps even sweeter. The New England Patriots were the heavy favorites to win the title in 2008. Down by four points with only a little over two minutes to play, Eli engineered an exciting final drive that took the Giants 83 yards down the field. The capper was passing for the winning touchdown. Many people believe that Eli earned his MVP trophy based mainly on his determination during that drive.

OTHER NOTABLE HONORS

Although Archie never made it to the big game, he did receive a number of other personal honors throughout his years in the NFL. He was named the league's MVP in 1978, and he made it to the Pro Bowl two years in a

David Tyree catches Eli's pass during a fourth-quarter drive that gave the Giants the 2008 Super Bowl title.

row, in 1978 and 1979. The Pro Bowl is a game that is played by NFL standout players from each conference. Fans vote for their favorite and most accomplished players. Peyton is a three-time league MVP and a nine-time Pro Bowl selection. In 2005, he took home the Pro Bowl MVP trophy. Eli made his Pro Bowl debut in 2009.

In addition to his professional honors and awards, Archie has received numerous acknowledgements for his college football career. He was chosen as the quarterback for several honorary teams, including the SEC 25-Year Team, the All-South Team, and the Ole Miss Team of the Century. In 1992, Archie was named Mississippi's All-Time Greatest Athlete. He has also been inducted into numerous halls of fame. The Saints have honored Archie by prominently featuring his name on the team's Wall of Fame.

Eli celebrates after throwing the winning touchdown pass in the 2008 Super Bowl.

Chapter Four

At Work, On the Field and Off

Archie, Peyton, and Eli Manning certainly have had an interesting and eventful past. Thanks to a number of current activities and associations, the present is also very rewarding for them. And as fate would have it, their future looks pretty bright as well.

Football has been the driving force for the Manning family practically since young Archie joined his first peewee squad in Drew. The game is more than a pastime; it's also the family business. Peyton and Eli are still active in the business. During football season, they lead their teams as starting quarterbacks. Meanwhile, Archie—who retired from playing in 1984—keeps his connection to the game. Instead of being on the field, Archie now works games from a broadcasting booth.

Each man has also made his successes in the sport work for him as well. The Mannings have been able to use their fame and popularity to help raise awareness and money for a number of worthy causes.

Easing into Retirement

By the time 1985 rolled around, Archie Manning had been playing professional football for 14 years. He was 36 years old. Football is a pretty rough sport. It takes an increasingly difficult toll on a person's body as he ages. Plus, Archie had been prone to injury his entire career. When he reported

These days, Archie is not just a New Orleans Saints commentator. He is also one of the team's biggest fans, cheering just like anyone else in the crowd.

to training camp with the Minnesota Vikings in 1985, he was nursing a torn hamstring and an elbow injury. He was also starting to have thyroid trouble.

One day after practice, the coach called him into his office and suggested that he retire. Rather than being upset, Archie was a little relieved. He didn't like the idea of being a backup quarterback, and he missed spending time with his family back in New Orleans. So before the season started, Archie called a press conference and announced his retirement. He then headed home.

Archie's love of and enthusiasm for football has never retired, though. Today, he works as a radio broadcaster, commentating for Saints games. In 2001, he also signed on as a television analyst for the CBS network's coverage of college football. In addition, Archie frequently works as a motivational speaker. He discusses business and personal management, as well as the principles of success. Stories surrounding his experiences playing football often make their way into his speeches as examples of the points that he is trying to get across to the audience.

In 2008, Archie became the chair of the National Football Foundation and College Football Hall of Fame. He has been a board member of the organization since 1994.

STILL IN THE GAME

Archie likes to attend the games in which his sons play. In the fall of 2009, Peyton entered his 12th season passing and calling plays for the Colts. Amazingly, even after all of these years, his popularity has not faded. And Peyton is not just a hero in Indiana. His talent as a quarterback and sense of humor, including a willingness to make fun of himself, has made him likable even in cities that support their own NFL teams. Even the *Boston Globe*, the hometown newspaper of Indianapolis' archrivals, the New England Patriots, admits that "America loves Peyton Manning."

MANNING PASSING ACADEMY

Archie, Peyton, and Eli have found yet another way to make football a part of their lives. In the off-season, the Manning men (including Cooper) join forces to share their love for and knowledge of the game. The Manning Passing Academy is a camp that teaches high school–age youngsters and future NFL wannabes the art of throwing a perfect spiral. The camp is at Nicholls State University in Thibodaux, Louisiana. Players in other offense positions, such as wide receivers and running backs, also learn a thing or two at the academy.

In true Manning fashion, motivation and sportsmanship are also stressed during the four-day camp. College and professional players and coaches are invited to the camp as guest speakers.

Cooper plays the triple-intended receiver for his father and brothers during a photo shoot for the Manning Passing Academy.

Meanwhile, Eli has entered his fifth season with the Giants. His popularity has always been something of a roller-coaster ride. New York fans first booed him at the 2004 draft, when he was picked by the Chargers. They then cheered when news of the trade was announced. That's pretty much how people have reacted to Eli throughout his pro career—at least until he and the Giants won the Super Bowl.

Since 2004, college football's Sugar Bowl Committee has presented the Manning Award, given to the year's outstanding collegiate quarterback. The award is named in honor of Archie Manning, seen here during the award presentation to Louisiana State quarterback JaMarcus Russell.

Winning the big game has put Eli in another light. Even more impressive than winning is that he had led the Giants to victory by taking down a powerhouse team that had been unbeaten all season long. No longer is he simply Peyton's little brother or someone who should have done better because he is a Manning. Eli is a quarterback who has earned a Super Bowl ring because of his own determination and skill. Football fans everywhere love and respect him for that.

In 2009, Eli signed a contract extension with the Giants. As reported in an August 6, 2009, *New York Times* article, the multiyear deal would give him the highest average annual salary in the NFL. Giants coach Tom Coughlin said, "He's been our leader, he's put all the time in, his attitude has been superior. He does everything he can on and off the field. He's a true Giant."

ENDORSEMENTS

Once they have become famous or noteworthy in their chosen sport, many athletes are hired to sell products and services. When an athlete or celebrity supports, promotes, or becomes associated with a product, he or she is said to endorse it. Therefore, a contract to sell an item is known as an endorsement.

Each of the Mannings has had or currently has endorsement deals. In his playing days,

Archie had a number of endorsements with businesses in the New Orleans area, including car dealerships and banks. The local offers kept coming in even after he had retired. On a national scale, Archie teamed up with the United Parcel Service (UPS) in 1971 to present the "Delivery Intercept Challenge." Archie was the company's spokesperson for the contest, where amateur players submitted video footage of astounding interceptions.

Peyton is the Manning who has the biggest and most numerous endorsements. A recent survey conducted by the online journal *Sports Business Daily* has indicated that, in the sports world, Peyton is second only to golfer Tiger Woods when it comes to mass appeal and the ability to sell products. Companies that have hired Peyton to represent them include Sprint, Sony, MasterCard, Gatorade, and DIRECTV. Nabisco also signed both him and Eli to appear in commercials for the company's Oreo brand cookies.

Eli started getting an increased number of endorsement deals as it became apparent that his team would go to the Super Bowl in 2008. In addition to the Nabisco spots with Peyton, Eli has been featured in national ads for Citizen Watch, Reebok, and ESPN Radio.

COMMUNITY SERVICE AND CHARITY WORK

Besides football, there is another area in which Archie has led by example. The Mannings are big believers in giving back to the community. Archie has been heavily involved in charity and service work for years. In fact, volunteering has become something of a second career for him. The majority of Archie's efforts benefit organizations in Louisiana and Mississippi.

A list of the organizations to which Archie and his wife, Olivia, donate their time looks like a "who's who" of nonprofits. Among them are the Boy Scouts, Special Olympics, 4-H, the American Heart Association, the American Cancer Society, and the United Way. For 25 years, Archie has hosted golf tournaments in Louisiana and Mississippi that raise money for cystic fibrosis.

The Peyton Manning Scholarship, awarded to exceptional high school student-athletes who enroll at the University of Tennessee, is just one way the Mannings have found to give back to the community.

Following in their father's footsteps once again, Peyton and Eli have also given their time and money to help those in need. In 1999, Peyton established the PeyBack Foundation, which provides out-of-school activities and various essentials, such as warm clothing, to disadvantaged kids. Winner of the NFL's Byron White Humanitarian and Walter Payton Man of the Year awards, Peyton also coaches flag football games and spends time with foster children through Indiana's Court Appointed Special Advocates program. His generous donations have made the Peyton Manning Children's Hospital at St. Vincent's a reality.

Eli also has a medical facility named in his honor, the Eli Manning Children's Clinics at the University of Mississippi Medical Center. He has served as an American Heart Association representative in New Jersey and works with the American Red Cross. Other causes that have touched his heart include AIDS awareness, human rights, and disaster relief. When Hurricane Katrina hit New Orleans in 2005, he and Peyton caught a flight to their hometown and volunteered for recovery missions.

Whether it's leading a football team or sharing their lives with others who are less fortunate, the Mannings are passionate about all that they do. That is the main quality that makes them the first family of American football.

1949

Archie Manning is born in Drew, Mississippi, on May 19.

1968

Archie enrolls at the University of Mississippi. He starts playing football the following fall.

1971

Archie is drafted to play for the New Orleans Saints.

1976

Peyton Manning is born in New Orleans, Louisiana, on March 24.

1978

Archie plays in the first of two back-to-back Pro Bowls. He receives the NFC Offensive Player of the Year award.

1981

Eli Manning is born in New Orleans, Louisiana, on January 3.

1985

Archie retires from professional football.

1988

Peyton begins playing football in the seventh grade at Isidore Newman.

1994

Eli begins playing football in the eighth grade at Isidore Newman. Peyton enrolls at the University of Tennessee.

1997

Peyton wins the Johnny Unitas Golden Arm award, given to the year's outstanding college quarterback.

1998

Peyton is the number one draft pick and is chosen to play for the Indianapolis Colts.

1999

Peyton makes the first of nine Pro Bowl appearances.

2003

Peyton wins his first of three NFL MVP awards. Eli is named Offensive MVP at the Cotton Bowl and wins the Johnny Unitas Golden Arm award.

2004

Eli is the number one draft pick and is chosen to play for the San Diego Chargers. He is later traded to the New York Giants.

2005

Peyton is named Pro Bowl MVP.

2007

Peyton and the Colts win Super Bowl XLI. He is named game MVP

2008

Eli and the Giants win Super Bowl XLII. He is named game MVP.

2009

Eli makes his first Pro Bowl appearance.

GLOSSARY

conference A group of sports teams that is divided by geographic division.

cornerback A football player who is on defense, covering receivers to make sure that they don't catch passes from the quarterback.

cystic fibrosis An inherited life-threatening disease that starts in infancy and causes severe lung damage and digestion problems.

déjà vu An instance in which present events seem as if they have happened before.

draft A system that lets teams pick new players from college ranks.

dynasty An important family or group that stays on top for several generations.

eligible Qualified or officially able to participate.

endorsement The support or promotion of a product or service.

Heisman Trophy An award given to the individual who is voted the best college football player of the year.

peewee league An amateur, organized version of a sport for young children who do not play for a school or other group.

Pro Bowl An annual game featuring the best professional football players from each of the teams in both conferences.

redshirting The practice of letting a player practice with a team but not play in games; it also extends a college player's eligibility.

scout An employee of a professional sports team who travels around the country looking for talented athletes.

SEC Southeastern Conference, a league of college teams that competes in various sports, including football.

sidelined Kept from participating; left on a football field's sidelines.

spinal stenosis A disease that narrows the spinal column and affects nerves in a person's arms and legs.

tendonitis When tendons become inflamed, or swollen, due to overuse or misuse.

trade To exchange one thing for another; in the NFL, teams make deals to trade players for other players or cash settlements.

varsity The main team that represents a school in organized sporting events.

winning season A season when a team has more wins than losses.

Manning Passing Academy

P.O. Box 10161

Eugene, OR 97440

(541) 302-4565

Web site: http://www.manningpassingacademy.com

Run by the Manning family, the academy teaches the fundamentals, techniques, skills, motivation, and sportsmanship necessary for success in the sport of football.

National Football Foundation's College Football Hall of Fame

111 South St. Joseph Street

South Bend, IN 46601

(800) 440-FAME (3263)

Web site: http://www.collegefootball.org

Established in 1951, the College Football Hall of Fame also functions as a museum and information resource on college football.

NFL Canada

47 Colborne Street, Suite 401

Toronto, ON M5E 1P8

Canada

(416) 322-0280

Web site: http://www.nflcanada.com

NFL Canada handles all of the National Football League's business interests in Canada.

PeyBack Foundation

6325 North Guilford, Suite 201

Indianapolis, IN 46220

(877) 873-9225

Web site: http://www.peytonmanning.com

Run by Peyton and the rest of the Manning family, the PeyBack Foundation was established to promote the future success of disadvantaged young people by assisting programs that provide leadership and growth opportunities for children at risk.

Pop Warner Little Scholars, Inc.

586 Middletown Boulevard, Suite C-100

Langhorne, PA 19047

(215) 752-2691

Web site: http://www.popwarner.com

This nonprofit organization provides young people ages 5 to 16 with football, cheer, and dance programs in 42 states and several countries around the world.

Pro Football Hall of Fame

2121 George Halas Drive NW

Canton, OH 44708

(330) 456-8207

Web site: http://www.profootballhof.com

This organization honors individuals who have made great contributions to professional football. It also safeguards professional football's historic artifacts and documents.

WEB SITES

Due to the changing nature of Internet links, Rosen Publishing has developed an online list of Web sites related to the subject of this book. This site is updated regularly. Please use this link to access this list:

http://www.rosenlinks.com/sfam/mann

FOR FURTHER READING

Buckman, Virginia. *Football Stars*. Bel Air, CA: Children's Press, 2007.

Christopher, Matt. *On the Field with . . . Peyton and Eli Manning*. London, England: Little, Brown, 2008.

Doeden, Matt. *Eli Manning* (Sports Legends and Heroes). Minneapolis, MN: Twenty-First Century Books, 2008.

Doeden, Matt. *Peyton Manning* (Sports Legends and Heroes). Minneapolis, MN: Twenty-First Century Books, 2008.

Hudson, Hugh. *Back-to-Back: Super Bowl Champions Peyton and Eli Manning*. New York, NY: Price, Stern, Sloan, 2008.

Jacobs, Greg. *Everything Kids' Football Book*. Cincinnati, OH; Adams Media, 2008

Madden, John. *John Madden's Heroes of Football*. New York, NY: Dutton Juvenile, 2006.

Marcovitz, Hal. *The Manning Brothers: Superstars of Pro Football*. Broomall, PA: Mason Crest Publishers, 2008.

Polzer, Tim. *Peyton Manning: Leader On and Off the Field*. Berkeley Heights, NJ: Enslow Publishers, Inc., 2009.

Sandler, Michael. *Eli Manning and the New York Giants: Super Bowl LXII*. New York, NY: Bearport Publishing Co., 2008.

Smithwick, John. *Meet Peyton Manning: Football's Top Quarterback*. New York, NY: PowerKids Press, 2007.

Stewart, Mark. *Indianapolis Colts*. Chicago, IL: Norwood House Paper Editions, 2007.

Worthington, Joe. *The Mannings: Football's Famous Family*. Mankato, MN: Red Brick Learning, 2005.

BIBLIOGRAPHY

Chappell, Mike. "Super Natural." *Sports Illustrated for Kids*, December 2005, Vol. 17, Issue 12, pp. 24–30.

Christopher, Matt. *On the Field with . . . Peyton and Eli Manning*. London, England: Little, Brown, 2008.

Furman, Phyllis, and Carrie Melago. "Eli Manning Piling Up Endorsements." *New York Daily News*, January 20, 2008. Retrieved April 2009 (http://www.nydailynews.com/sports/football/giants/2008/01/20/2008-01-20_eli_manning_piling_up_endorsements.html).

JockBio.com. "Eli Manning." 2008. Retrieved April 2009 (http://www.jockbio.com/Bios/EManning/Eli_bio.html).

JockBio.com. "Peyton Manning." 2008. Retrieved April 2009 (http://www.jockbio.com/Bios/Manning/Manning_bio.html).

Lapointe, Joe. "Giants See the Value of a New Manning Deal." *New York Times*, August 7, 2009, p. B15.

Lawrence, Andrew. "Manning Up." *Sports Illustrated for Kids*, September 2008, Vol. 20, Issue 8, pp. 22–24.

Lopresti, Mike. "The Other Manning Brother Lives a Life Without Regret." *USA Today*, January 30, 2008, p. C6.

Manning, Archie, and Peyton Manning, with John Underwood. *Manning: A Father, His Sons, and a Football Legacy*. New York, NY: HarperCollins Publishers, Inc., 2000.

Morris, Wesley. "Mr. Popularity." *Boston Globe*, October 14, 2007, p. E1.

Polzer, Tim. *Peyton Manning: Leader On and Off the Field*. Berkeley Heights, NJ: Enslow Publishers, Inc., 2009.

Quinn, T. J. "Proud Papa." *New York Daily News*, January 8, 2006. Retrieved March 2009 (http://www.nydailynews.com/archives/sports/2006/01/08/2006-01-08_proud_papa__in_manning_famil.html).

Sandler, Michael. *Eli Manning and the New York Giants: Super Bowl XLII*. New York, NY: Bearport Publishing Co., 2008.

Tuchman, Rob. "Archie Manning Q & A." *Incentive Magazine*. Retrieved April 2009 (http://athletes-celebrities.tseworld.com/tuchmans-blog/2008021219/archie-manning-qandampa-with-rob-tuchman.php).

Worthington, Joe. *The Mannings: Football's Famous Family*. Mankato, MN: Red Brick Learning, 2005.

ABOUT THE AUTHOR

Jeanne Nagle is a writer and editor who lives in upstate New York. Her longstanding interest in sports and admiration for the Manning family have led to the diligent research that informs this book. Among the books she has written for young adults are *Careers in Coaching, Frequently Asked Questions About Wii and Video Game Injuries and Fitness,* and *What Happens to Your Body When You Swim.*

PHOTO CREDITS

Cover (left), pp. 4–5, 26 © Paul Spinelli/Getty Images; cover (center), p. 23 © James Flores/NFL Photos/Getty Images; cover (right) © Tami Tomsic/Getty Images; p. 8 © Art Shay/Sports Illustrated/Getty Images; pp. 9, 12–13, 33 © Bill Frakes/Sports Illustrated/Getty Images; pp. 15, 34–35, 37 © AP Photos; pp. 18–19 © Streeter Lecka/Getty Images; p. 20 © Ronald Martinez/Getty Images; p. 25 © Vincent Laforet/Allsport/Getty Images; p. 28 © Donald Miralle; p. 29 © Al Tielemans/Sports Illustrated; p. 31 © Al Messerschmidt/Getty Images.

Designer: Les Kanturek; Editor: Kathy Kuhtz Campbell;
Photo Researcher: Marty Levick